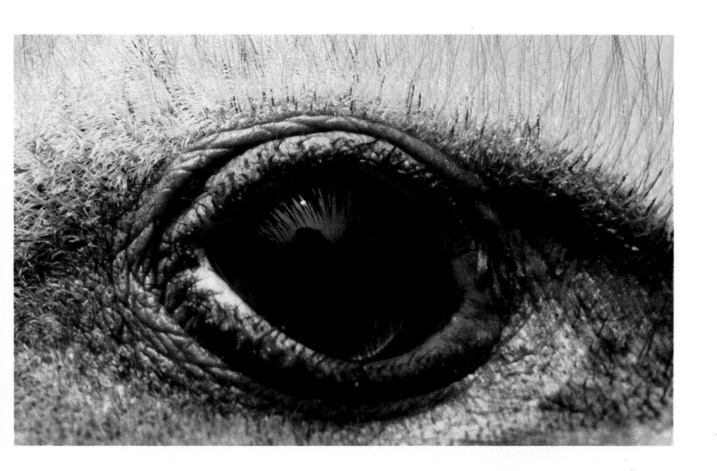

# WALK WITH YOUR EYES

*Text and Photographs by*
MARCIA BROWN

# WALK WITH YOUR EYES

FRANKLIN WATTS | NEW YORK | LONDON | 1979

TO KENNETH MALY
May he delight in looking

Library of Congress Cataloging in Publication Data

Brown, Marcia.
    Walk with your eyes.

    SUMMARY: Text and photographs encourage
the reader to carefully observe his surroundings.
    1. Visual perception — Juvenile literature. 2.
Consciousness — Juvenile literature. 3. Imagination
— Juvenile literature. [1. Perception] I. Title.
BF241.B74            158            78-27688
ISBN 0-531-02925-5 lib. bdg.
ISBN 0-531-02385-0

We can see
from the time we are born.
But looking—
that's something else.

Looking is
    walking through your eyes
    to a new world.

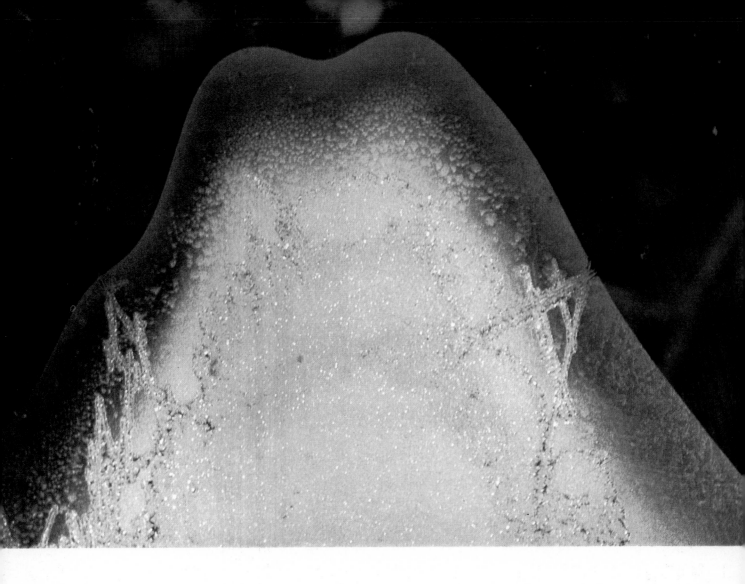

Walking takes time
    to feel every bump,
    and every tickle.

You can
    climb a crystal mountain
    on a winter window.

Explode
    with a dandelion
    in the summer sun.

Looking can be
    seeing with a lens
    that makes little
    look big...

    or lets you be
    small as an ant.

Ask a ladybug
why she hugs
a daisy.

*This jeweled beetle*
*feasting on our garden,*
*he's a tourist from Japan.*

Take a ride
on a dragonfly.

Looking can be
    flying
    with someone else's wings —

feeling
the beat of the rain
on the face
of a flower—

watching
a spider mending her web,
torn by the rain.

Stre-e-etch
your brand-new
leaf wings

and take off
in the first wind.

*After the picnic*
*the old swing in the pines,*
*the lake upside down!*

Looking can
turn the world
head over heels,
when *you* are—

or on its side, if *you* are.
Then you see
things you never saw before.

A swan father
ready to protect
his nesting mate.

Looking can choose.
    Roll up a sheet of paper.
    Look through the tube.
    See just what you want to see.

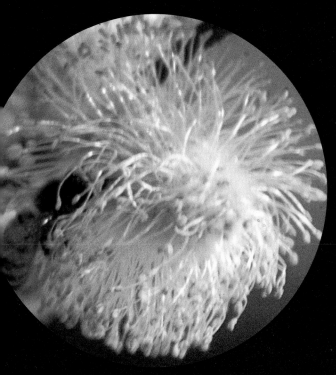

A pussy willow
with long hair.

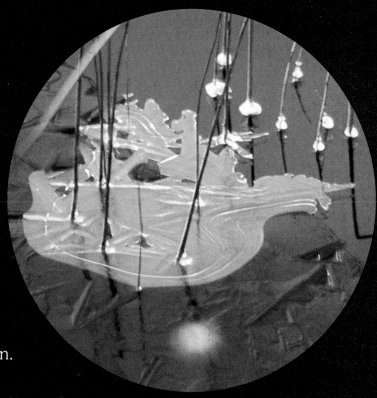

An ice duck
going after ice corn.

A tiny frog
popping up to say,
"Who's there?"

Looking can
invite you
to someone's party.

Looking
   lets you hear
   what others say.

Looking
    lets you go
    anywhere you want to.


You can
    pole a lily pad
    across a pond

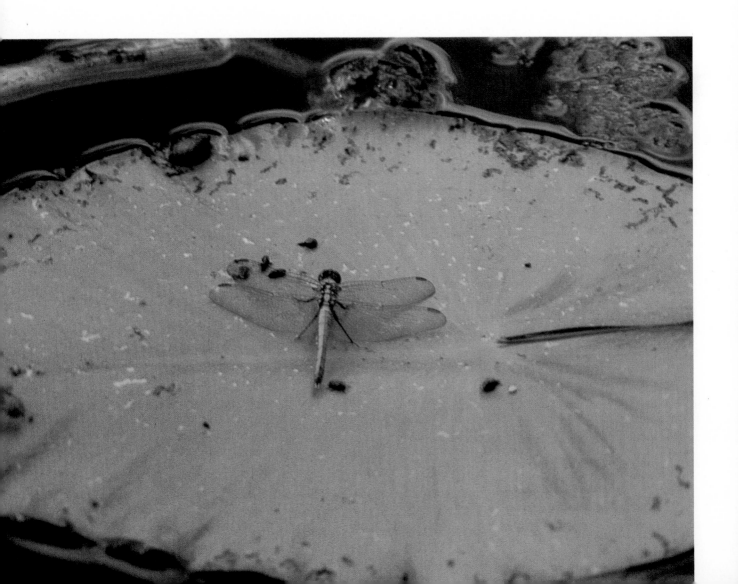

and say
"Good morning!"
to a frog.

You can
slide down
the green glass curve
of a wave —

or hide
in a cave of kelp.

A leaf map
can show you
where.

Looking tells you
Who was here?

Who lives there?

What happened?

*The crash of the wave*
*sends the small snails tumbling.*
*Sand scrawls tell the tale.*

Which way does the current flow?

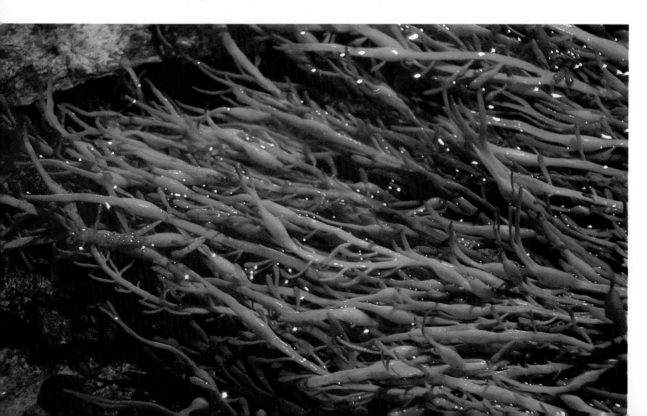

Looking makes you ask,
Why does the robin's nest
hold only one baby?

Looking lets you
   do anything!

You can
   sit under a canopy
   of diamonds.

   Pick your wand
   on a frosty morning.

Collect
ice elephants
for your zoo.

Grin right back
at a water monster.

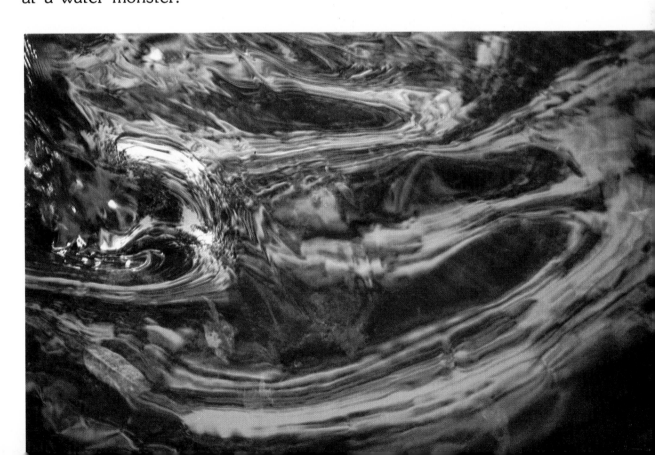

Looking is a way
        to store up good things
    to remember.

Spring can sing
its green song
to you in December.

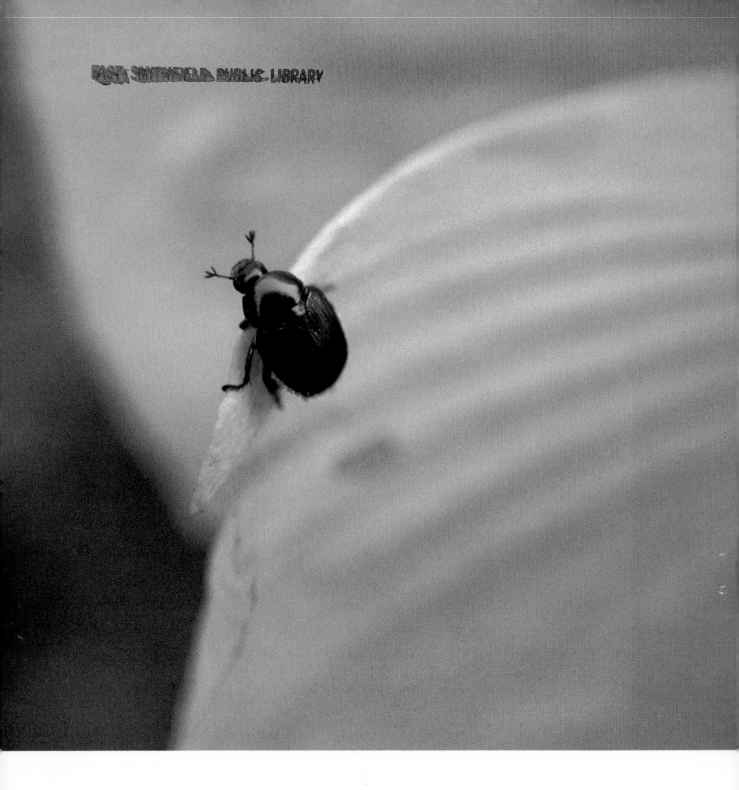

Look over the edge
    of your world.
    Let your eyes do the walking.

    You can
    make what you see
    your own.